FOUR SIMPLE WORDS

A Starting Point for New Christians

Todd Wallace

IN MEMORY OF Mr. Francis Hinkle, a man whose life said more about love than any words could.

1

Love

Matthew 22:34-40

But when the Pharisees heard that Jesus had silenced the Sadducees, they gathered themselves together. One of them, a lawyer, asked Him a question, testing Him, "Teacher, which is the great commandment in the Law?" And He said to him, "YOU SHALL LOVE THE LORD YOUR GOD WITH ALL YOUR HEART, AND WITH ALL YOUR SOUL, AND WITH ALL YOUR MIND. This is the great and foremost commandment. The second is like it, YOU SHALL LOVE YOUR NEIGHBOR AS YOURSELF. On these two commandments depend the whole Law and the Prophets."

There is a twofold concept that is the basis for all of Christianity. It is simple, yet it is weaved throughout the entire Bible.

Love God. Love people.

Everything you are, everything you do, everything you think, and everything you learn must be inspired by and measured by those four simple words.

Everything.

2

History

To give you some perspective on why it is important that Jesus came as a sacrifice to pay for our sin you need to know how sin came into the world and understand the history of God's people. From the moment that sin came into the world, God had a plan to deal with it. Nothing takes God by surprise. God and Jesus have both called themselves I AM. Notice that it's not I WAS or I WILL BE. God is eternal. He has always existed and will always exist. He is conscious of all past and future events. While He gives you the freedom to make choices, He already knew what those choices will be before you were born. Knowing all that, He still sent His Son to pay for each of our sins. He did this because He loves us.

Let's start at the beginning.

Genesis 1:1-3

In the beginning God created the heavens and the Earth. The Earth was formless and void, and darkness was over the surface of the deep, and the Spirit of God was moving over the surface of the waters. Then God said, "Let there be light"; and there was light.

John 1:1-5

In the beginning was the Word, and the Word was with God, and the Word was God. He was in the beginning with God. All things came into being through Him, and apart from Him nothing came into being that has come into being. In Him was life, and the life was the Light of men. The Light shines in the darkness, and the darkness did not comprehend it.

Genesis is the first book of the Old Testament of the Bible. The Bible begins with the verses above from the book of Genesis. John is one of the four books called the Gospel which begin the New Testament of the Bible. It is a common misconception that Jesus didn't enter the picture until the New Testament. However, He was with God in the beginning. He has been the Word of God all along. You'll also notice that the Holy Spirit has been in the Bible from the beginning as well.

God the Father, God the Son, and God the Holy Spirit are the three parts of one being that is God. They created the universe, including Earth. God created man and shortly after created woman to be a partner with man. He gave them the whole world to rule over with only one exception. They were not to eat from the tree of the knowledge of good and evil. Adam and Eve disobeyed God and this is how sin was first introduced into the world.

Abraham was a descendant of Adam. He was faithful to God. God told Abraham that He would make a great nation come from him, but Abraham and his wife were already quite old. The promise was kept and Abraham had two sons. Isaac was the son God had intended to carry on the line of Abraham. As Isaac grew old, he passed an inheritance unto his son Jacob. Later in life, God changed Jacob's name to Israel.

Israel was the father of twelve sons which became twelve great tribes of the nation of Israel which still exists to this day. Joseph was the favorite son of his father Israel. He ended up being sold by his brothers into slavery in Egypt. God favored Joseph and made him second in command to Pharaoh, the leader of Egypt. During a period of famine, Israel moved his family to be in Egypt with Joseph. Over the next four hundred years the twelve tribes of Israel grew to be between one and two million people.

By this time, the Pharaohs of Egypt had long since forgotten about Joseph and had enslaved the nation of Israel. A baby named Moses ended up being given to the daughter of the current Pharaoh. Moses grew up in the royal household. When he found out about his ancestry, he became angry about how they were being treated. After killing a slave master he fled. God spoke to Moses and told him to go to Pharaoh and demand the release of God's people. It took 10 plagues, sent by God, before Pharaoh let the nation of Israel leave Egypt. They fled into the wilderness.

God gave Moses Ten Commandments for the nation of Israel to follow. By the time Moses got down the mountain with the commandments, the people had already constructed a gold idol, which broke the very first commandment. This was the beginning of centuries of sin and disobedience.

Eventually God gave Moses the full set of laws for Israel to follow. These were not only their legal system, but also rules for the construction of the tabernacle which was the tent they used to worship God, and how to deal with the sins of the twelve tribes of Israel. The Law was given to Moses in great detail and it was used for hundreds of years to govern the nation of Israel.

Remember, by this time there were well over a million people in the nation of Israel. That would be an impossible number of people to provide food and water for. They wandered in the desert for forty years and God provided for the needs of his people.

God promised to give Israel a land to call their own. Through great struggle they found and conquered the land which became the country we now call Israel. In the beginning it was ruled by a series of Judges. During this time the people kept cycling through sinning against God by worshipping idols, being conquered and oppressed, remembering and calling out to God, and then God would send a Judge to deliver them.

The people decided they wanted to be ruled by Kings. God allowed this and sent prophets to anoint the Kings of Israel. Most of the Kings ended up failing God and the people. One of the few great Kings was named David. He had his faults and did commit some huge sins, but he had a heart that truly loved and worshipped God. David wrote the book of Psalms which are full of songs and poems that worship God. David's son Solomon asked God for wisdom to rule Israel. God granted his request. While Solomon ruled Israel, he built the temple to God in Jerusalem.

A civil war eventually divided the nation of Israel into the northern kingdom of Israel and the southern kingdom of Judah. About the time that the Assyrians took control, the prophet Isaiah began speaking prophesies about a Messiah that would come in the future to redeem Israel as their King. As the Babylonians came to power, the prophet Jeremiah spoke of a new covenant that would come and God would write the Law on the hearts of men.

Throughout this period, most of the Kings of Israel were evil men who turned away from God.

The entire northern kingdom was lost. The southern kingdom of Judah only survived because eight of their twenty-eight kings were faithful to the Lord. Eventually they were taken out of Judah and into captivity in Babylon. God spoke through Jeremiah and told the people to be patient and they would be returned to their land in seventy years.

Forty-six years later, when Persia had conquered Babylon, Cyrus allowed the Jews (named for their kingdom Judah) to return to the land God had given them. Zerubbabel, a descendant of King David, brought some of the Jews back to Israel which was in ruins. They rebuilt the temple in Jerusalem. The temple was completed exactly seventy years after the Jews had been taken into captivity in Babylon. God gave the people a few more prophets over the next 50 years.

Then there were 400 years of silence.

3

Prophecy

There are over 300 prophecies in the Bible about the Messiah. Here are a few from Isaiah and one from Jeremiah. Remember, these prophecies were made hundreds of years before the birth of Jesus.

Isaiah 7:14 (The virgin birth of Jesus)

Therefore the Lord Himself will give you a sign: Behold, a virgin will be with child and bear a son, and she will call His name Immanuel (meaning God is with us).

Isaiah 9:6 (A son called God)

For a child will be born to us, a son will be given to us; and the government will rest on His shoulders; and His name will be called Wonderful Counselor, Mighty God, Eternal Father, Prince of Peace.

Jeremiah 23:5 (A descendant of King David)

"Behold, the days are coming," declares the Lord, "when I will raise up for David a righteous Branch; and He will reign as king and act wisely and do justice and righteousness in the land."

Isaiah 35:5-6 (He will perform miracles)

Then the eyes of the blind will be opened and the ears of the deaf will be unstopped. Then the lame will leap like a deer, and the tongue of the mute will shout for joy. For waters will break forth in the wilderness and streams in the desert.

Isaiah 53:3-4 (He will be rejected)

He was despised and forsaken of men, a man of sorrows and acquainted with grief; and like one from whom men hide their face He was despised, and we did not esteem Him. Surely our griefs He Himself bore, and our sorrows He carried; yet we ourselves esteemed Him stricken, smitten of God, and afflicted.

Isaiah 53:5-6 (He will die for our sins)

But He was pierced through for our transgressions, He was crushed for our iniquities; the chastening for our well-being fell upon Him, and by His scourging we are healed. All of us like sheep have gone astray, each of us has turned to his own way; but the Lord has caused the iniquity of us all to fall on Him.

Isaiah 53:7 (He will be silent before his accusers)

He was oppressed and He was afflicted, yet He did not open His mouth; like a lamb that is led to slaughter, and like a sheep that is silent before its shearers, so He did not open His mouth.

Isaiah 53:8 (He will pay the price for our sins)

By oppression and judgment He was taken away; and as for His generation, who considered that He was cut off out

*of the land of the living for the transgression of my people,
to whom the stroke was due?*

Isaiah 53:9 (He will be buried in a rich man's tomb)

*His grave was assigned with wicked men, yet He was with
a rich man in His death, because He had done no violence,
nor was there any deceit in His mouth.*

Isaiah 50:6 (He will be spat on and beaten)

*I gave My back to those who strike Me, and My cheeks to
those who pluck out the beard; I did not cover My face
from humiliation and spitting.*

Isaiah 49:6 (Salvation will reach the ends of the Earth)

*He says, "It is too small a thing that You should be My
Servant to raise up the tribes of Jacob and to restore the
preserved ones of Israel; I will also make You a light of the
nations so that My salvation may reach to the end of the
Earth.*

4

Life

God gave a girl named Mary a baby. She conceived the baby as a blessing from God without being with a man. God arranged for her to have a husband named Joseph whom He told about the baby being a gift from God. While the people around them did not understand, Mary and Joseph knew that they would be parents to someone very special.

Mary and Joseph were from Nazareth in Israel. They had to go to Bethlehem, the city of their ancestor king David, so they could be counted in a census being taken by the Roman government. While they were in Bethlehem, the baby was born. He was named Jesus. His birth was announced by angels from heaven singing his praises.

Jesus grew up much like everyone else. His father worked as a carpenter and his mother loved Him. From a young age He began to grow in wisdom and was favored by God and men. His cousin

John the Baptist had been preaching a message about the Messiah coming soon. Jesus came to John and was baptized in water before beginning his ministry on Earth.

When He began his ministry, Jesus gathered twelve men to teach and have fellowship with. They came from all walks of life. They were witnesses of His love and of miracles He performed. Jesus travelled around Israel loving people and healing their bodies and their spirits. His twelve disciples learned about how God loves each person on Earth.

The religious leaders among the Jewish people observed Jesus. Some began to understand that He was the fulfillment of prophesies in the scriptures. Others did not believe and challenged Jesus. They saw Him as a threat to their position and plotted to get rid of Him. Jesus knew what they were planning. He knew what was in their hearts. While He spoke only truth to them, their hearts and minds were closed and they did not understand. However, they were never able to find evidence against Jesus because everything He said was righteous and true.

It is important to understand that God sent his son Jesus to Earth for a purpose. That purpose was to redeem all of humanity from sin. It was going to be fulfilled by Jesus being sacrificed on a Roman cross. Jesus tried to explain to his disciples that He was going to be put to death on a cross and then He would come back to life in three days. What He was telling them was too difficult for them to believe.

Jesus went to the temple, the home of his Father God. It had become a place where merchants sold animals to be used for sacrifices and money lenders exchanged things for money that could be paid to the temple. It had become a perversion of God's original intent for making sacrifices and offerings to Him. With righteous anger Jesus became riotous. He overturned the tables of the money lenders and drove them out of the temple with a whip.

This was finally what the opponents of Jesus needed. They were able to use this event as evidence that Jesus challenged Roman authority. When the Roman governor Pilate questioned Him, Jesus barely spoke and did not speak at all while He was being accused. He had to submit to being beaten and crucified to fulfill his mission on Earth. If He had spoken in His defense, the truth would have set Him free. While the charges were not true, they did end up getting Jesus crucified on the cross. God placed the sins of the entire world from all time, yes even yours, on Jesus. He died as a sacrifice paying the price for all of our sins.

One of the religious leaders who did believe in Jesus, Joseph of Arimathea, donated his personal tomb for Jesus to be buried in. The entrance was covered by a huge stone that took three men to move. Those who opposed Jesus convinced the Romans to put guards at the stone because they knew that Jesus had said He would rise from the grave.

The disciples scattered because they were afraid of being hunted down for being followers of Jesus.

Three days passed.

An angel came and opened the tomb where Jesus was buried. Jesus did indeed rise from the grave, just as He said He would. He visited with His disciples and many other people. He told them that He would be going to Heaven soon and that His Father God would be sending a helper to Earth called the Holy Spirit. He instructed the disciples to take His message to the ends of the Earth.

The Holy Spirit was given to the disciples to help them remember everything Jesus told them and to teach them. It is still available to us today.

5

The Good News

Wouldn't it be nice if life came with an instruction manual? With all of its twists and turns, ups and downs, joys and sorrows it would be great if every baby came with a set of instructions on how to raise them and how to perform maintenance and upkeep throughout their life. Even better, how about throwing in a lifetime warranty just in case life gets broken?

Guess what. God did give us an instruction manual. It's called the Bible. He also gave us a lifetime warranty, which is salvation through His Son Jesus.

The Bible is a collection of sixty-six books and letters collected throughout Jewish and Christian history. Written by more than forty people across fifteen hundred years, it is one continuous story that is still being lived out today. The Bible started with the creation of everything, continues through the first sin of mankind, through the history of

God's chosen people, includes messages about God sending a savior to redeem the world from sin, the arrival of that savior, His teachings, His sacrifice for our sin, the creation of the church, and a message about Jesus coming back to establish a final kingdom on Earth. Within this story are life lessons that cover every aspect of human existence. People have spent their lifetime studying the Bible and still find new lessons within it. It was written for real people having real challenges and struggling with real sin.

Because of sin, we all deserve to be punished. It creates a debt that we have no way of paying. Fortunately Jesus came to Earth to pay that debt for us. He did this because God loves us. Most people can imagine giving their life for someone else. Some might actually do it. Who could imagine giving the life of their child to save someone else? Even more than that, who could imagine giving the life of their child to save the worst, most despicable person on Earth? God did. He didn't send His Son to save the good, the mostly good, or the people that deserve a second chance. He gave His only Son for each and every person in the world. He gave His only Son for you. Imagine the worst thing you have ever done. Yes, that thing. Focus on the thing that just flashed in your mind. Now imagine Jesus walking up to you on that day saying, "I love you. You are mine. I am redeeming you from this." That is exactly what He did.

He paid the price for that sin and all of your other sin by becoming the final blood sacrifice. Here is where we get it backwards. We often think that we have to earn His forgiveness, or that we have to constantly be on guard against slipping up and losing his forgiveness. What we fail to understand is that the debt is already paid. Nothing we can do will ever be able to repay the price He paid for you. Whether or not a person ever accepts the gift of salvation, the price has already been paid. Jesus is just waiting on us to accept the gift.

Often the best day of our life comes right after the worst day of our life. One day, everything is wrong and falling apart. The next day we give that whole mess to Jesus to sort out, and then we're free. That doesn't mean all of our problems are immediately solved. It does mean that we are now free from our sin and we have a God who promises to be with us through good times and bad. Since God can only speak truth, those promises can be counted on.

Once you've acknowledged that Jesus is your savior your new life begins. It will be a lifelong journey of growth and discovery. You're going to discover who God is, what you mean to Him, and who you can become through salvation and the gift of the Holy Spirit.

Keep an open mind. Many times we come to a new situation in life with preconceived notions about the way things or people should be. There is a difference between knowing your mind and having your mind made up. It is good to know what you believe and why you believe it. Be open to the possibility of learning something new and having a new, better informed opinion. Do you still remember those four simple words from Chapter 1?

Love God. Love people.

Everything you are, everything you do, everything you think, and everything you learn must be inspired by and measured by those four simple words.

Everything.

6

The Bad News

It's time for the bad news. You are going to mess this up.

Big time!

Often.

And it's OK.

It's important that you understand this. No person on Earth can be righteous in their own strength. No one can. If it were even remotely possible we would not need the sacrifice that Jesus made for us. We do need Jesus. The Holy Spirit can change your life. It is a process. God can handle everything life throws at you. It takes time to build up trust. In the meantime, you will stumble. You will do stupid things. It's not an excuse for your behavior, but it will not make God love you less. He already knows where you're going to fail. Just keep dusting yourself off and coming back to His love.

There is another side to this coin. You can't do a single thing to earn God's love. You can't do a single thing to pay Jesus back for your salvation. No matter how much of the Bible you read every day, how many minutes or hours you spend praying, or how much money you toss in an offering plate, you aren't going to make a dent in the debt. There are two reasons for that. First, if you try to wrap your mind around the enormity of what Jesus did for you, any attempt to repay it would be an insult. Second, if you have accepted your salvation through Jesus, the debt is already paid. It no longer exists for you.

Temptation will never leave you. The most committed ministers, the worship leaders in every church, and men and women who have been walking with God for decades all face temptation. Even Jesus faced temptation while He was here on Earth. Of all people who have ever lived, Jesus is the only person who spent an entire life without giving in to temptation. Think of all of the billions of people who have ever lived. One. Only one was able to make it through life without sin, and I'm sorry to say it wasn't you. It won't be you.

It is a good thing for us that God had a plan for this all along. He sent His Son to rescue us. Because of our sinful nature we are prone to giving in to temptation. Sin is in this world and we can't escape it by ourselves. God gave us tools to combat temptation. They are training and trust. Jesus faced temptation by quoting Scripture. We can study the Scripture and do the same. Reading the Bible daily trains us how to deal with the struggles in life. For the most part we learn how to trust God.

Jesus faced temptation by trusting His Father. While on Earth, Jesus was a man and He repeatedly demonstrated that He is subject to His Father's will. God loves His children. As His children we have to learn to trust Him. This comes through experience. Trust starts with prayer. Let God know what you're thankful for. Let God know what you need. He already knows, but He wants to be the one to provide it for you.

Not all of us were born into families where our parents wanted us, where we were expected, where we were loved. Take heart. You do have a Father that is not of this world. He has wanted you since before you were born. He has been expecting you to arrive. He loves you. He wants amazing things for you. He wants to become everything that is good in you.

Eventually you can be filled by His Holy Spirit. It will guide and direct your life in powerful ways. At this point, temptation will still be there, but it will have a much harder time even getting your attention. With the Scripture written on your heart and well established trust in God, temptation won't stand a chance.

And even then, should you stumble, God loves you. Dust yourself off and come back to his love.

7

Give Up

It's time to give up.

Now isn't that contrary to everything we've been taught? The little engine didn't give up. Winston Churchill urged his nation to never give up. We see it time and time again. We fight to the last man. It seems to define who we are. We teach our children that they can accomplish anything. We tell them not be a quitter, don't give up, and never surrender.

This way of thinking has allowed us to accomplish great things in this world. We live in a free country because our ancestors didn't give up. Our achievements in science, agriculture, architecture, business, and industry only exist because people didn't give up.

Many of us fight for our families. We do whatever it takes to feed them and clothe them. We make sure they are provided for and healthy. We stay up nights worrying and get up early to get to work.

There is nothing we wouldn't do to take care of our own.

It all rests on our shoulders. We're tough as nails. We can handle anything. We are the masters of our fate.

Or are we?

Jesus submitted. He submitted to the will of His Father and came to Earth to die for us. He submitted to His human parents here on Earth. He submitted to serving those He was sent to lead. He submitted to persecution by those who should have welcomed Him. He submitted to being beaten and spat upon. He submitted to the most extremely painful and degrading execution possible. He achieved victory through submission.

It takes a great deal of strength to surrender.

By surrendering to Jesus we allow Him to save us. By surrendering our lives and everything in them to God we allow Him to provide for us. By surrendering to the Holy Spirit we allow Him to lead us.

We are encouraged to trade any and every part of us for what God offers. If you are in need of wisdom, you can try and get by on the wisdom of men or ask God for his wisdom. If you are in need of giving or receiving compassion, God can help with both. Love? God is love. Every facet of love can be learned and experienced by surrendering to God. Give Him your marriage. Give Him your children. Give Him your community. Give Him your broken relationships with friends and family. Need forgiveness? You're coming to realize that He's the foremost expert in the world on that subject.

Sometimes the will of God will take us through hardships. A sickness may lead you to someone who needs to be loved. A death may draw a family together and heal broken hearts. A lost job may mean moving your family to a new town with a church that needs a new youth pastor. Surrendering your life to God means giving Him the good and the bad. He says that He causes all things to work together for good to those who love Him, to those who are called according to His purpose.

Of course surrender comes down to trust. The more we learn to trust God the more we are able to surrender to Him. We learn to trust God by having a relationship with Him. That relationship is developed through reading the Bible and conversing with God through prayer. The better we get to know God the easier it is to trust Him. As we become aware of how God provides for all of our needs, we learn to trust Him more. By thanking God for what He provides and worshiping Him we express that trust. Eventually we reach a tipping point where we can give everything over to Him.

All we have to do is surrender to Him.

8

The Last Resort

Here's a tip for you. It's a shortcut that will rapidly progress your faith and your walk with God. Welcome to the fast track. Many Christians have missed this and it took them a long time to realize they missed the mark. This is not a secret, but it can be the secret to your success.

God is not the last resort.

Prayer is not what you do when all else has failed. God is not who you call when everyone else has failed you. You don't have to wait until you've tried everything in your own power to overcome your circumstances. God doesn't want you to prove that you can handle life by yourself. He only wants you to prove one thing, that you trust Him.

There is only one time where God is the last resort, and it's the last time He should be your last resort. That is the moment you came to ask Him into your life and to forgive you of your sins. At that point you had probably tried everything and everyone else. You realized that nothing and no one else was going to be able to deliver you from sin. While that is still true, you know better now. There is no need to wait until your life is falling apart to approach God.

Often we will overhear someone saying, "All we can do now is pray." God instructs us not to worry. He says to seek Him and His righteousness first. Not last. Not when all else fails. He is ready, willing, and quite able to take care of our needs.

Trusting God should be our first response. It should be a way of life. We should pray constantly praising Him, thanking Him, and letting Him know what we need. Keep in mind that Jesus prayed to His Father all the time. He asked for His Father's will to be done. So should we.

If you get in the habit of trusting God for the small things in your life your faith will be strong when it comes time to trust God for something bigger. You might have been able to handle that small thing, but God might have been planning to turn it into a blessing for you. Every action we take and every decision we make can be inspired by God. Lift up everything you do to God. Let Him be a part of your life. God wants to provide for us. We need to let Him.

The alternative is a life of fear. God doesn't want us living a life of fear. You have a choice to live a life of desperation calling on God as a last resort or a life of faith where you rest in the promises that God has made to take care of you. Making the decision now, before things get tough, will prepare you for things to come. Start praising God for small victories. Thank Him for His provision and worship Him as Lord of your life. Keep in mind that fear and praise cannot occupy the same space.

Our problems can bury us making it hard to see a way out. We know our strength and our weakness. At times our problems appear to be unsolvable by God or by man. That only means that you've forgotten who God is. God created the universe, all of it. That is the scope of God. Now look at the precision of God. He knows how many hairs are on your head. He has the power to speak any and everything into existence, and He loves you.

9

Pray

So what is prayer?

We tend to take prayer for granted, even though we don't rely on it enough. We are free to pray to God every moment of every day. It hasn't always been that easy.

In the Old Testament prayer was conducted by the priests of the tabernacle. The tabernacle and later the Temple had an area called The Holy of Holies. It is important to understand how sacred the Holy of Holies was. It was a place that people were not allowed to go as it was the inner sanctuary where God dwelt. There was a veil made of layers of curtains three feet thick that separated God from humanity. One day per year the High Priest would sanctify himself and enter the Holy of Holies. The purpose of this annual visit was to ask for atonement for the sins of the nation of Israel. Normal people were not allowed to do this. It was reserved for the High Priest and only the one day per year.

By the time Jesus was walking the Earth, priests would pray in the synagogue and on street corners. These were demonstrations of the false righteousness of the priesthood. John the Baptist had been teaching his disciples how to pray directly to God. The disciples of Jesus asked Him to teach them to pray like John was teaching his disciples.

Matthew 6:9-13

"Pray, then, in this way:

Our Father who is in heaven,
Hallowed be Your name.
Your kingdom come.
Your will be done,
On Earth as it is in heaven.
Give us this day our daily bread.
And forgive us our debts,
as we also have forgiven our debtors.
And do not lead us into temptation,
but deliver us from evil.
For Yours is the kingdom
and the power and the glory forever.
Amen."

Jesus taught his disciples, and us, the manner in which we should pray. The prayer He offered was a demonstration that we should acknowledge who God is, that we view Him as Holy, and that we pray to complete His will. Then He instructed that we ask for daily provision and ask for forgiveness of sin. We are also instructed to forgive others. That was followed by acknowledgement that only God can keep us safe from temptation and evil. In closing He affirmed that God is Lord over everything. This doesn't mean that we have to pray this exact prayer. Jesus gave His followers a model for prayer because something extraordinary was going to happen soon.

Jesus told this parable, which is a short story that is intended to make a point.

Luke 18:10-14

"Two men went up into the temple to pray, one a Pharisee and the other a tax collector. The Pharisee stood and was praying this to himself: "God, I thank You that I am not like other people: swindlers, unjust, adulterers, or even like this tax collector. I fast twice a week; I pay tithes of all that I get." But the tax collector, standing some distance away, was even unwilling to lift up his eyes to heaven, but was beating his breast, saying, "God, be merciful to me, the sinner!" I tell you, this man went to his house justified rather than the other; for everyone who exalts himself will be humbled, but he who humbles himself will be exalted."

You might notice that the acceptable prayer wasn't something fancy. It didn't rhyme or use big words or some ancient way of speaking. It was an honest plea from a man to his God.

Everything Jesus did on Earth had a purpose. He taught his disciples, the ones who were going to carry his teaching to the rest of the world, how to pray. It was a preparation for what was about to happen. Jesus knew He would be crucified soon. The moment that Jesus died, the heavy three foot thick veil in the Temple was completely torn in half. This was significant. Now there is no separation between God and humanity.

We are now able to speak to God directly.

10

The Bible

You might find yourself asking why there are so many versions of the Bible. If they were all translated from the same source, shouldn't they say the same thing?

Yes and no.

The original Bibles were in Hebrew, Aramaic, and Greek. If you've ever experienced speaking another language, you'll understand that there are differences in language and culture that don't translate well. There are three types of Bible translations. Each has their purpose.

Word for Word translation Bibles attempt to keep the meaning of the translated words as close to the original words as is possible while still constructing legible sentences. This can make the Bible more difficult to understand and may leave it open to misunderstandings of cultural differences. However, they are more accurate and faithful to the original text. These are also called Literal Translations.

Thought for Thought translation Bibles attempt to update the grammar and style of the Bible in a manner that makes it easier to read and understand. This is an attempt to balance understanding and accuracy. These are also called Dynamic Equivalent Translations.

Paraphrase translation Bibles attempt to maximize understanding at the expense of accuracy. They use the ideas of the original text but are not bound to accurately communicate the original words in the text. Paraphrased Bibles are going to be easy to understand, but will not be reliable for deep Bible study. They are not technically translations since they rely on the author's own words. These are also called Free Translations. That has nothing to do with the cost of the Bible, but how liberal they have been with the translation.

Here are some of the Bibles that fall into each category. There are many more translations available, more than could be listed here. These are some of the most popular.

Word for Word
KJV - King James Version
NKJV - New King James Version
NASB - New American Standard Bible

Thought for Thought

NRSV - New Revised Standard Version
NIV - New International Version
NLT - New Living Translation

Paraphrased

GNT - Good News Translation
TLB - The Living Bible
MSG - The Message

The most accurate translation is the King James Version. The New Kings James Version and the New American Standard Bible have updated their words and grammar into more modern English while staying as close as possible to the original text. Many people use Thought for Thought translations for their daily Bible reading because they can understand what they are reading and they trust that the translation is still relatively accurate. People use the Paraphrased Bibles when they are trying to understand the general story of the Bible and to read verses in the most modern English possible.

Eventually you might want to try something like a Parallel Bible. This type of Bible puts two translations side by side. This promotes both the accuracy of something like a Word for Word Bible with the understanding of something like a Paraphrased Bible. A good combination would be a New King James Version along with The

Message. It's like reading the original text with a translator sitting next to you.

This book uses the New American Standard Bible in all quoted verses. It is highly accurate but more readable than the King James Version.

If someone has given you a Bible, that's great. Thank God that someone has cared about you and given you such a valuable gift. However, it's important that you find the Bible that's the right fit for you. The more you study the Bible, the closer you get to God. The closer you get to God, the more you'll want to study the Bible. People are more likely to study a Bible that they're comfortable with.

When you are presented with Bible verses, it is easy to take them out of context. What this means is that by themselves the verses sometimes seem to mean something that wasn't intended. The best thing to do is to read the entire chapter, or at least the entire paragraph that contains the verse. This helps to ensure that you are getting the correct meaning of the verse.

11

Where to Start

There are sixty-six books in the Bible. It has over 750,000 words. It's not in chronological order but arranged by type, so reading it cover to cover can be a bit odd. Where should you start? There are hundreds of suggestions out there on where to start reading the Bible. Here is one suggestion.

Since the odds are you are not a Jew who is converting to Christianity, termed a Messianic Jew, it is not necessary to begin with the Old Testament. Of course, a Messianic Jew would already be intimately familiar with the Old Testament. Please understand that the Old Testament is just as important as the New Testament when studying the Bible. However, since you do not share the history of the Jews, nor have you been required to keep the Laws of Moses, the Old Testament is not really a good starting place. You should return to it later.

Start with the Gospels in the New Testament. They are the books Matthew, Mark, Luke, and John. Matthew, Mark, and Luke are called the Synoptic Gospels. This means they tell relatively the same stories told in relatively the same manner. The content of John is different but is still about the life of Jesus. John just contains a different set of stories. It omits many of the stories told in the other three Gospels and includes additional stories that are not in the other three Gospels. A good way to look at this is that it supplements the other three Gospels.

The Gospels begin with the birth of Jesus. They tell a little bit of his early life and then pick up right before his ministry begins. For the most part, they describe the ministry of Jesus on Earth including how and why He came to offer Himself as a sacrifice for each of us.

Once you finish with the four Gospels, read the book of Acts also known as The Acts of the Apostles. It is the story of the early church. It begins after Jesus had been crucified and raised from the dead by God. It describes what is known as Pentecost when God delivered his Holy Spirit to us to guide and teach us. Then the book follows the apostle Paul as he visits Jewish synagogues, which are places of worship, and tells them of the Gospel of Jesus. Some receive his message well and some do not. After visiting the Jewish people in each city, Paul takes the message to the non-Jews called Gentiles. Again, some receive the message well and some do not.

Beyond Acts are letters written to many of the early churches. You should continue reading through these letters. However, in addition to what you're reading at this point there is another book you should read. It is not a complete Bible translation. It is called The Story. It uses material from the New International Version which is a Thought for Thought Bible translation and tells the story of the Bible in chronological order. The Story is abridged. This means it has been shortened by leaving out some parts. Here's what The Story can do for you. It can give you the big picture of what is included in the Bible. It lays out the entire history, and some of the future, of God's plan for us.

Once you've finished The Story and the letters to the early churches, the New Testament ends with the Book of Revelation. You will be somewhat familiar with it if you have completed The Story. If not, you might want to engage with a mentor before tackling the final book of the New Testament. It is the prophecy of the apostle John about the end of the current Earth and the establishment of God's kingdom on Earth. Much of the content is figurative and is the subject of much debate since the events have not happened yet. It can be heavy subject matter that is better suited to being discussed with an experienced mentor. If you decide not to read the Book of

Revelation at this time, or if you have completed it with a mentor, it's time to go back and work on reading the Old Testament.

Speaking of studying the Word of God with other people, this set of suggestions is for your personal reading, studying, and growth. You should also be studying the Bible with a group of people in the church. This may include attending church on Sunday as well as Bible studies held during the week.

12

The Church

Church attendance is not required for salvation. Please don't read that as, "don't go to church," or that "church isn't important." While attending church is not required for salvation, belonging to the church is a vital part of your walk with God.

We often visualize a building when we speak of the church. While many church buildings exist, there is a big difference between a church building and the church that the Bible teaches about. Jesus spoke of us as his body. Also notice that we're not talking about belonging to this church or that church. We're talking about belonging to THE church. The body of Christ is THE church. The church is comprised of compassionate people who love each other in the name of Jesus.

The purpose of the church according to Ephesians 4 is to help us grow from being children in our faith into maturity. All of the parts of the body of Christ should work together for the growth of the body and to build itself up in love.

Many churches today have adopted Acts 2:42 as a kind of motto. Immediately after the Holy Spirit was delivered to the apostles, Peter preached a sermon and 3,000 people received their salvation. These new Christians asked Peter what they were to do. He instructed them to get baptized and receive the gift of the Holy Spirit. Once they had done so, this is what they did next.

Acts 2:42

They were continually devoting themselves to the apostles' teaching and to fellowship, to the breaking of bread and to prayer.

The church is a gathering of people who come together to study the Word of God, to spend time with people who care about each other, and to pray with and for each other.

Not only will belonging to the church help you understand the Bible, attendance brings with it many other benefits. Keep in mind it's not all about you. Do you remember Chapter 1? What were those four simple words?

Love God. Love people.

Attending church helps you be encouraged in your walk with God. You can have the most rotten week. The moment you walk into your church it becomes easier to focus on God and what He means to you. That's not to say you can't focus on God throughout the week. You most certainly should be. But there is something about gathering together with your church family that strengthens that focus. Speaking of your church family, many of them have been struggling through their week and could use a word of encouragement from you. Talk with them about their life. Express your concern and help encourage their walk with God.

Church services begin with music. You're encouraged to sing along. This isn't a talent competition. It's an opportunity to worship your God. He gave you your voice. Express your love for Him with it. Your praise and worship is a sweet sound in His ear. God's love is a two way street. The more you express your love for Him, the more you are able to receive the vast amount of love He has for you. The greatest thing about the love of God is that it's meant to be shared. Love the people in your church. They are your brothers and sisters in Jesus. People who think they have it all together don't come to church. The people who make up your local church realize that they are broken and only saved through the grace of God. They are people who need to be, and appreciate being loved.

If you have needs, your church will pray for you. It can be hard to ask for help. We often let our pride get in the way. People in the church understand that God is the only one who can truly meet our needs. Be that person yourself. When your brothers and sisters in Jesus ask for prayer then pray with them or for them. Don't just mention a prayer in church and go on with your life. Remember them through the week. Hold them up in prayer every day. And while this might sound backwards, pray for the leadership of your church. While it might look like it comes easy to them, caring for the needs of your local church body is a heavy burden.

The church is the perfect place to bring your family, or to start one. The closer a husband and wife get to God, the closer they get to each other. The deeper your love is for God, the deeper your love can be for each other. The stronger your relationship is with God, the stronger your relationship can be with each other. If you have, or plan to have children church is vital. There are two sides to the coin. The church will teach your children Bible stories and life lessons from the Bible. This is a good thing. However, they will find the example you set more meaningful than any Bible story. When they see you growing in your faith it helps them believe they can grow in their faith. Talk with your children about what you are learning and ask them about what they are learning. It will build strong bonds within your family.

Finally, even if none of the other benefits above were valid, we come to the most important reason to attend church. God will be there.

13

Ten

The subject of tithing is a difficult one for churches. It is challenging for the leader of a church to stand in front of people and say that it is good and right for you to pay a portion of your income to the church without looking like the church is just out to get your money. The truth of the matter is that the tithe is not between you and the church; it is between you and your God. You are not purchasing your salvation with it. Salvation is a gift that cannot be purchased. You are not buying a better place for yourself in Heaven or on Earth. A sacrifice is being given to God by an obedient servant who loves Him. It is an acknowledgement that you belong to God and that you recognize that all material wealth in your life has been given to you by God.

In Genesis 4 we read the story of Cain and Abel, two of the children of Adam and Eve. They offered sacrifices to God. Cain offered fruits of the ground and Abel offered the firstlings of his flock. God was pleased with Abel's offering and was displeased with Cain's. This story didn't end well since Cain killed his brother Abel. However, it does demonstrate that people have been giving offerings to God since the beginning.

Later in the book of Leviticus, Moses introduced the Law and with it regular tithing to the Tabernacle of God. Tithe means one-tenth or ten percent. The people of Israel were to give ten percent of their food and livestock to support the Tabernacle and the tribe of priests who worked there. Later when Solomon built the Temple in Jerusalem, the same Law applied and the Jewish people continued to tithe, even at the time Jesus walked the Earth.

Jesus had some issues with how the tithe was being handled by the priesthood of his day. He ended up becoming riotous in the Temple, overturning the tables of the money lenders, and driving them out of the Temple with a whip. Tithing had become big business when it was meant to be worship and submission to God.

Once the church was established they didn't speak of tithing in the traditional sense. Remember that tithe refers to one-tenth or ten percent. At this time, the people joining the church sold everything they owned and gave it all to the church to be distributed as people had need. Since they were making communal living arrangements, it was right that they all support one another.

Today we no longer live in church communities where we share everything. Most local churches have a building with its own set of expenses which is led by a full time minister. The members of the church each live in their homes with their families. They go to a workplace and earn money to be spent on food and shelter for their family. From this provision, which ultimately came from God in the first place, we give a tithe or ten percent to the church. While the funds are used to support the church and to minister to the community, the act of giving is a deeply personal experience between the giver and God.

For most people, money is a difficult idol to overcome. Money tends to rule us. Being wealthy can become a false sense of salvation. "As long as I make enough money I'll be ok. If I have a million dollars in the bank I can ride out any storm. With enough money I'll be safe. I don't have to bother God with my needs. I can take care of myself." And you can take care of yourself. It will be a lonely, isolated existence, but you can certainly live there. Where is the love? Where is the relationship with God?

It is easy to look at the rich and say that they have become servants of acquiring wealth. Keep in mind that the less money you have, the more likely you are to be a slave to it. When you have difficulty paying your bills or putting food on the table worry and guilt can rule your heart. Money becomes everything you think about. It decides what you do with your day. It decides the amount and quality of time you spend with your family. It becomes a strain on your marriage, often to the point of destroying it. Money is a bully.

So what are we to do? How do we break the chains of enslavement that money has placed us in?

Give it away.

Those without money will say, "That's easy for people who have money. They have plenty to give away." Those with money will say, "That's easy for people who don't have much. They don't have to give much." Both those statements are true. But that's not the point.

When you give money away, it loses its power over you. The chains break. This is true whether you're giving money to the church or you've given it to a charitable cause. Either way you end up with broken chains.

This is where relationship comes into play. When you recognize that everything that is provided in your life comes from God you will understand that everything was his to begin with. By giving the first ten percent of everything you receive back to God, you are formally acknowledging that He is the ruler in your life and that money is not. The moment you make that decision and you actually do it for the first time, you experience something.

It is liberating.

It comes down to ownership. Everything belongs to God. Let's take a step backwards in time to the beginning of human life.

Genesis 2:7

Then the Lord God formed man of dust from the ground, and breathed into his nostrils the breath of life; and man became a living being.

God made us. We belong to Him. The very air we breathe comes from God. From His very breath we were created. We return that breath to Him through worship. It is a cycle. Breath was given to us and breath is returned to Him.

Everything in our lives is a gift from God. Our family, our home, our job, our clothes, our car, our furniture all came from Him. We have these people and things in our life by the grace of God. Yet He still owns them.

Taking a portion of what God has provided for us and returning it to Him is our acknowledgement that He is the one we belong to. It reinforces our belief that He is the one who provides for us.

14

A God Shaped Hole

This chapter is completely an observation of humanity and our need for God. It is not supported by verses in the Bible. Consider it an essay on the human condition.

Throughout all of human history, mankind has displayed an inherent need for deity. Every culture worships something greater than itself.

There seems to be a God shaped hole inside every person. We were built by God to worship Him and to receive his love. Then we are supposed to pass His love on to other people. We are a vessel built specifically for that purpose.

When we don't have God in our lives, we attempt to fill this hole with other things. In the Old Testament, these things were referred to as idols. Originally these were physical idols representing false deities that God's people would look to when they had forgotten about Him. Today, we don't find many physical idols. However, the meaning of the word idol now includes false ideas and representations. Of that, we have plenty.

Before we understand that God is what should fill our God shaped hole, we recognize that the hole is in us and we try to fill it ourselves. We are quite creative in what we try to fill it with.

Some try to fill the hole with material things. Fashion is a big one to many people. They have to have the finest, newest clothing. Cars fill the dreams of many people. Whether it's the newest sports car or the most posh minivan, automobiles are often worshipped. It could be homes, boats, or model train sets that are distracting people from worshipping God.

Others turn to self when they notice the hole. This can start at a young age when getting good grades defines who they are. As they get older, they stack up degrees and define their worth through their titles. Power and prestige can be an alluring idol. One idol that is most often discussed is wealth. Many bow to the almighty dollar. Jesus once had a discussion with a rich young ruler who was doing everything else right but just couldn't give up his love for wealth.

Many people have fallen victim to addictions. These are a dangerous and destructive set of idols that take the lives of many people before they are able to escape. Most people think of addictions being limited to drugs, alcohol, and gambling. However, people get addicted to activities like shopping, sex, video games, plastic surgery, food, and using the internet. The phrase adrenaline junkie suggests that these risk takers are addicted.

Here's where it gets even trickier. If we recognize that the hole is God shaped, we have to ask ourselves a question. How big is God? This hole in us is bigger than we are, much bigger. The desire to fill the hole with idols and addictions is limitless. If left unchecked, our tendency to fill this hole consumes us. The object of our worship becomes who we are. When people meet us they think of us as the drug addict, the car guy, or that rich lady.

The hole is too big for anything else to fill other than God. The only way to get rid of our idols is to fill the hole with God and let Him push the things we have replaced Him with out of our life. The way we do this is through reading the Bible and through prayer. The Bible explains who God is. We get to know who He is by studying the Bible. That gives you knowledge of God. To have a relationship with Him, you have to communicate with Him. That comes with prayer. The more you speak with God through prayer, the stronger your relationship becomes.

God built us well. When we recognize that God belongs in the hole we can start filling the hole with Him. Since this God shaped hole is bigger than us, eventually we are filled with more of Him than we are of us. People will begin to look at you and see God. At this point we become compelled to love people. It's not a question of choice. We have fulfilled our purpose and become a vessel for God's love to flow through us and reach other people.

15

Grace

Before you can understand grace, you have to understand that God loves you. His grace is completely defined by the depths of his love for you. So how much does God really love you?

The Bible is full of references to how much He loves you. Let's go with one that's probably familiar to you. John 3:16 is probably the most quoted Bible verse ever.

John 3:16

For God so loved the world, that He gave His only begotten Son, that whoever believes in Him shall not perish, but have eternal life.

First off, the chapter on the Bible discussed the various translations and how they can be worded differently. However, in almost all translations this verse begins with, "For God so loved the world." It doesn't say, "God loved" or, "God kind of loved." It says God SO loved.

The next section says, "That He gave His only begotten Son." By gave, we know it means He allowed His Son to be brutally sacrificed for you. With full foreknowledge of what was going to happen, he sent His Son to Earth to pay for your sin. He purchased you back from sin with the blood of His dearly beloved Son.

And finally it closes with, "That whoever believes in Him shall not perish, but have eternal life." Whoever? That means that everyone gets a chance. That means that you get a chance. What do you get a chance at? You get a chance at eternal life. God wants you to live with Him…forever.

The book First John (1 John) is a different book of the Bible than the Gospel of John. It speaks of us being called children of God.

1 John 3:1

See how great a love the Father has bestowed on us, that we would be called children of God; and such we are. For this reason the world does not know us, because it did not know Him.

For those of us who have accepted Jesus as our Lord and savior, God claims us as His children. We know how much He loves His firstborn son Jesus. Imagine how much He loves His other children. Imagine how much He loves you.

Ephesians 2:8-9

For by grace you have been saved through faith; and that not of yourselves, it is the gift of God; not as a result of works, so that no one may boast.

Grace is undeserved compassion and blessing. It is not something that has been earned. Grace is a gift from God. Not only does it not need to be repaid, there is nothing in the world that you can do or possess that would equal the value of grace. The entirety of the Bible is a testament to the fact that humanity in no way deserves the grace of God.

God first demonstrated his grace for us by saving us from our sin. He continues to demonstrate his grace for us in our everyday life. The longer we walk with God, the less likely we will be to make mistakes. In the meantime, God allows us to make mistakes which are already paid for by the blood of Jesus. Does this mean that we can just go back to a life full of sin? It absolutely does not. It does mean that we have a gracious God who has offered us the ability to turn away from sin.

Titus 2:11-12

For the grace of God has appeared, bringing salvation to all men, instructing us to deny ungodliness and worldly desires and to live sensibly, righteously and godly in the present age...

God gave us the gift of the Holy Spirit. The more you let the Holy Spirit lead your life, the more you will be able to resist the temptation of sin. If you happen to fall, get back up, dust yourself off, and come back to His love and grace.

Grace is powerful and changes lives. We think of being graceful to those who deserve it. In our minds grace has to be earned with good behavior before it is offered. Lucky for us, God doesn't see it that way. He extended grace to those of us who could never have been worthy. Both Jesus and Stephen the martyr asked God to forgive those who were killing them. We can certainly show grace to those who don't deserve it.

Luke 6:35-36

But love your enemies, and do good, and lend, expecting nothing in return; and your reward will be great, and you will be sons of the Most High; for He Himself is kind to ungrateful and evil men. Be merciful, just as your Father is merciful.

The best way to show God how much you appreciate his grace is to offer it to other people.

16

Baptism

Baptism in water is a common practice. Some churches believe that full body immersion in water is required. Some believe that sprinkling water on the head is sufficient. Others don't believe that baptism is required at all. Jesus did not baptize anyone, most likely because He did not want to give people the opportunity to boast about being someone special who was baptized by Jesus Himself. However, Jesus was baptized by John the Baptist. Towards the end of his time on Earth, Jesus did instruct his disciples to go and baptize people in the name of Father and the Son and the Holy Spirit.

Matthew 28:19

Go therefore and make disciples of all the nations, baptizing them in the name of the Father and the Son and the Holy Spirit,

But why do we need to be baptized? Is it just symbolic or is there an actual purpose? The New

Testament is full of verses about baptism. What it comes down to is that it is an outward expression of what is happening inside of you. Peter describes it as an appeal to God to be cleansed and an acknowledgement that the cleansing is through Jesus.

1 Peter 3:21

Corresponding to that, baptism now saves you-not the removal of dirt from the flesh, but an appeal to God for a good conscience-through the resurrection of Jesus Christ,

In Paul's letter to the Romans, he goes into greater detail. The submersion in water represents the burial of Jesus in the tomb. The name of God is spoken as acknowledgement of who raised Jesus from the dead, and the body rises from the water as Jesus rose from the grave. This symbolizes the death of our old self which dies with Jesus and our rebirth as a new creation who is no longer subject to sin.

Romans 6:3-6

Or do you not know that all of us who have been baptized into Christ Jesus have been baptized into His death? Therefore we have been buried with Him through baptism into death, so that as Christ was raised from the dead through the glory of the Father, so we too might walk in newness of life. For if we have become united with Him in the likeness of His death, certainly we shall also be in the likeness of His resurrection, knowing this, that our old self was crucified with Him, in order that our body of sin might be done away with, so that we would no longer be slaves to sin;

Keep in mind that the act of baptism does not save you. The water doesn't save you. The symbolism is only telling a story. Submission to baptism is an expression of the salvation that you have already accepted. Salvation itself only comes from faith in Jesus.

Many people attend church and never give their lives to Jesus or accept his salvation. Asking to be baptized in front of the members of the church leaves no doubt that you have accepted the salvation of Jesus. In most things, God has instructed us not to act publicly for the glory of ourselves and to be praised by other people. For instance, giving to charity should be done privately and not in a manner that draws attention. However, baptism is not something to be done in private. There are two reasons for this. First, water baptism glorifies God in front of his people. Second, it lets the body of the church know that they have a new member who needs care and instruction.

17

The Holy Spirit

John the Baptist recognized Jesus for who He is. He had been baptizing people as a Jewish tradition of mikvah which was a spiritual cleansing. The mikvah was a preparation for a new beginning. John told his followers that another was coming after Him who would give them the Holy Spirit.

Matthew 3:11

As for me, I baptize you with water for repentance, but He who is coming after me is mightier than I, and I am not fit to remove His sandals; He will baptize you with the Holy Spirit and fire.

Jesus came to John for baptism right before beginning his ministry. He underwent the symbolic cleansing of the mikvah administered by John, who didn't feel worthy to carry the sandals of Jesus. After being baptized the Holy Spirit descended on Jesus.

Matthew 3:16-17

After being baptized, Jesus came up immediately from the water; and behold, the heavens were opened, and he saw the Spirit of God descending as a dove and lighting on Him, and behold, a voice out of the heavens said, "This is My beloved Son, in whom I am well-pleased."

Towards the end of his ministry Jesus was speaking with His disciples trying to prepare them for what was to come. They were understandably worried about Jesus not being with them anymore. To comfort them, He told them about the Holy Spirit who would be coming as a Helper. Remember that the Holy Spirit has been present since the beginning. Jesus tells the disciples that the Holy Spirit would be residing inside them. This must have been difficult for them to understand because prior to Jesus, God and man were separate.

John 14:16-17

I will ask the Father, and He will give you another Helper, that He may be with you forever; that is the Spirit of truth, whom the world cannot receive, because it does not see Him or know Him, but you know Him because He abides with you and will be in you.

Jesus instructed the disciples that one of the purposes of the Holy Spirit is as a teacher who would help them remember everything Jesus ever told them. This helped them spread the Gospel and eventually helped the books known as the Gospels to be written.

John 14:26

But the Helper, the Holy Spirit, whom the Father will send in My name, He will teach you all things, and bring to your remembrance all that I said to you.

We have access to the Holy Spirit today. He helps us learn who Jesus is and how much He loves us.

John 15:26

When the Helper comes, whom I will send to you from the Father, that is the Spirit of truth who proceeds from the Father, He will testify about Me...

After God raised Jesus from the dead, He went to His disciples. He told them that He could only stay with them for a short time, but reminded them that the Holy Spirit would be given to them. He instructed them to go and wait for the arrival of the Holy Spirit. Once He had ascended back to Heaven, the Holy Spirit came to the gathered disciples. Peter began to preach a sermon and three thousand people accepted the salvation of Jesus.

Acts 2:2-4

And suddenly there came from heaven a noise like a violent rushing wind, and it filled the whole house where they were sitting. And there appeared to them tongues as of fire distributing themselves, and they rested on each one of them. And they were all filled with the Holy Spirit and began to speak with other tongues, as the Spirit was giving them utterance.

So what does all of this mean to you? Not only does the Holy Spirit teach us about Jesus, it also helps us overcome temptation. There is an internal war between the flesh which is prone to sin and the Spirit which does away with sin.

Galatians 5:16-18

But I say, walk by the Spirit, and you will not carry out the desire of the flesh. For the flesh sets its desire against the Spirit, and the Spirit against the flesh; for these are in opposition to one another, so that you may not do the things that you please. But if you are led by the Spirit, you are not under the Law

In the beginning this will probably be uncomfortable. Your flesh is still going to want to sin. You will feel a strong desire to do what is right and good. Sometimes the flesh will win. This can bring on feelings of shame and guilt. This is perfectly normal. Every Christian goes through this. At this point you are a beloved child of God and have been forgiven for all of your sins by the finished work of Jesus. Just keep dusting yourself off and coming back to His love.

Galatians 5:19-21

Now the deeds of the flesh are evident, which are: immorality, impurity, sensuality, idolatry, sorcery, enmities, strife, jealousy, outbursts of anger, disputes, dissensions, factions, envying, drunkenness, carousing, and things like these, of which I forewarn you, just as I have forewarned you, that those who practice such things will not inherit the kingdom of God.

As you learn to overcome the flesh through the Holy Spirit, your Earthly desires will be replaced by the fruit of the Spirit. Sins of the flesh are in direct opposition to these things. It is wonderful that these things are also in direct opposition to sin. When the Holy Spirit brings these things into your life you will begin to desire the lasting fulfillment they bring more than you desire the temporary pleasures of sin.

Galatians 5:22-23

But the fruit of the Spirit is love, joy, peace, patience, kindness, goodness, faithfulness, gentleness, self-control; against such things there is no law.

Once you are filled with the Holy Spirit, you have become strong in your relationship with God and are beginning to understand how unknowable the depths of His love for you are. At this point in your walk with God, you will be compelled to share His love with other people. This will come in two forms.

You will share in God's love for people. You will want to help them in their need. This is not a desire to prey on their weakness and manipulate them into believing in God. It is a true and honest longing for their well-being. You will want to feed the hungry and put clothes on the homeless. You will want to visit the elderly and pray for the sick.

The second way God's love will manifest in you is an ability to see people who are looking. The hurt and broken people in the world are looking for something, for someone, for love. Most often they don't know what they are looking for. The Holy Spirit will open your eyes and your heart so you can recognize them. He will also give you the words to speak. They will be simple words of compassion. Start by listening to them. Don't have an agenda. Ask them about their life. Stop and listen to them. Then tell them what is on your heart. Tell them your story of four simple words.

This is the fulfillment of the two great commandments Jesus spoke of.

Love God. Love people.

18

A Collection

While you should certainly get started right away reading the four Gospels, you may want to explore the Bible a bit. Here is a collection of interesting stories and instructions to help you learn more about your faith. They are broken into Old and New Testament sections and kept in order as they are in the Bible solely for the purpose of being able to find them within your Bible. Please read any that draw your interest.

The Old Testament

Genesis 1-2: The Creation

In the first two chapters of the Bible we learn how God created the heavens and the Earth, all of the plants and animals, and the first man and woman.

Genesis 3: The Fall of Man

Adam and Eve commit the first sin. All of mankind must now live in sin. Adam and Eve are removed from the Garden of Eden.

Exodus 20: The Ten Commandments

Moses brings the Ten Commandments to the nation of Israel.

Psalm 23: The Lord, the Psalmist's Shepherd

This is one of the most well-known chapters in the Bible. It begins with, "The Lord is my shepherd, I shall not want.

Psalm 51: A Contrite Sinner's Prayer for Pardon.

The greatest king of Israel committed adultery and murder. God punished the house of David for his sins. This is King David's prayer for mercy and cleansing from his sin.

Isaiah 53: The Suffering Servant

Written 700 years before the birth of Jesus, this chapter describes who the Messiah will be in great detail. Every single piece of this prophecy was fulfilled.

Daniel 3: The King's Golden Image

Even under the very real threat of death, the story of Shadrach, Meshach and Abed-nego, is about three young men who were obedient to God and stood their ground.

Daniel 6: Daniel in the Lions' Den

Here is another story of a man who stood for God at great personal risk. The first half of the chapter describes why Daniel was thrown to the Lions. The second half of the chapter is a demonstration of God's provision.

The New Testament

Matthew 5-7: The Sermon on the Mount

This is the longest set of scripture in this list since it actually covers three full chapters. It is a sermon that Jesus preached. This sermon contains some of the most blessed teachings of Jesus.

Mark 12: Jesus Answers the Pharisees, Sadducees, and Scribes

Chapter 1 of this book comes directly from chapter twelve of the Gospel of Mark.

Luke 2: Jesus' Birth in Bethlehem

Commonly known as The Nativity, the second chapter of Luke is the story of the birth of Jesus. It describes how Mary and Joseph ended up in Bethlehem. Prophecy had decreed that Jesus would be born there.

Luke 15: The Prodigal Son

There are actually three parables in chapter fifteen of the Gospel of Luke. All three of them speak about God's love for us and that He longs to have a relationship with us. The third parable about a son who found his way back home is a favorite of many people.

John 14: Role of the Spirit

Chapter 14 of the Gospel of John ends with Jesus telling the disciples about the Holy Spirit that God would be sending to them after Jesus was gone.

John 20: The Empty Tomb

Jesus had repeatedly told his disciples that He would rise from the dead after three days. It was too much for them to comprehend, which is why He had previously told them it would happen so that when it did they might believe.

Acts 2: The Day of Pentecost

Pentecost is the day celebrating the day God gave the Law to Israel through Moses. On this day the disciples were gathered together and the Holy Spirit was delivered to them.

Acts 9: The Conversion of Saul

You might have heard of the apostle Paul. Before he was an apostle, his name was Saul. He was on a mission to exterminate the early church until Jesus changed his mission and his name.

Romans 8: Deliverance from Bondage

God's love is the topic of this chapter. It describes God's relationship to us as Father and our relationship as his children.

1 Corinthians 13: The Excellence of Love

The description of love in this chapter is a road map of how we should treat each other.

Colossians 3: Put On the New Self

Last but certainly not least, Colossians 3 instructs you how to behave as a Christian. There are words of encouragement for how to conduct yourself at work and at home.

About the Author

Todd Wallace is just a normal guy. While many Christian books are written by pastors, he wanted to write a book for everyday Christians by an everyday Christian.

Growing up an Army brat, he had been exposed to many different denominations of churches. When he left home, he also left the church. It took him a long time realize that leaving the church was a mistake. This is why the story of the prodigal son (Luke Chapter 15) is one of his favorites.

Now he is married to a wonderful woman and they are surrounded by four children. They have three beautiful daughters and an amazing son. When the girls were young and his wife was pregnant with their son, he realized that there was something missing from their life. It's funny how being responsible for other human beings reorganizes one's priorities.

The family started attending a great church, but it seemed like there was so much to learn. Coming back to the church after so long, Todd felt that his faith was like a complicated puzzle that needed to be put back together piece by piece. It took a long time to get to a place where everything seemed to fit together. He wrote this book in hopes that he could help other people come to an understanding of how the Bible is one continuous story of love.

While each person's walk will be different, perhaps this book can help you begin a good foundation of faith and a deep relationship with God. All you have to do is remember four simple words.

Love God. Love people.

www.ingramcontent.com/pod-product-compliance
Lightning Source LLC
Chambersburg PA
CBHW021140020426
42331CB00005B/845